WOLVES

Wildlife Monographs – Wolves
Copyright © 2006 Evans Mitchell Books

Text Copyright © 2006 Chris Weston
Photography Copyright © 2006
Art Wolfe and Chris Weston

Art Wolfe and Chris Weston have asserted their rights
to be identified as the authors and photographers
of this work in accordance with Section 77 of the
Copyright, Designs and Patents Act 1988
www.artwolfe.co
www.chrisweston.uk.com

First published in the United Kingdom in 2006
and reprinted in 2009 and 2012 by:
Evans Mitchell Books
86 Gloucester Place
London W1U 6HP
United Kingdom
www.embooks.co.uk

Design by:
Roy Platten at Eclipse
Roy.eclipse@btopenworld.com

British Library Cataloguing in Publication Data.
A CIP record of this book is available
on request from the British Library.

ISBN: 978-1-901268-18-8

Printed in China

WOLVES

ART WOLFE & CHRIS WESTON

Evans Mitchell Books

Contents

Introduction

No other animal evokes such strong emotion in humans as the wolf. From idolisation to repugnance, wolves have been at the extremes of man's consciousness from time immemorial. Our understanding of this complex creature, however, has grown along with a better understanding of animal science and our changing values towards the environment.

Wolves are one of the most successful animals ever to have existed on earth, a trait hewn from an ability to adapt to new environments, seemingly at will. They are able to do so because of a symbiosis with their environment that we are only just beginning to understand.

Despite persecution, wolves remain uncategorized in the IUCN Red List of endangered species due to the extent of available habitat, recognition of wolves' remarkable ability to readily adapt to new environments. Of all Earth's habitats, only rainforests and true deserts are impervious to the wolf.

As our knowledge of wolves grows in substantiality, so we are learning that the animal we were once quick to denigrate and eradicate shares far more of our traits than we have ever given it credit for. My interest in wolves began after spending time with an habituated pack in North America. I was transfixed by the discipline within the pack, the sophistication of their language and their dedication to the community, not the individual. Ever since I have studied and photographed them with a passion.

Essentially this is a book about wolves, but it is also a story about us and our role in the bigger picture. For when writing about wolves it is impossible to ignore the impact that humans have had on their history and the part we have yet to play in their future.

History of the Wolf

Many thousands of years ago, man and wolf lived in harmony, mutual predators in wild lands. Then, around 5,000 BC, to protect domestic livestock, mass killing of wolves was commonplace and our relationship altered dramatically. Wolves became our enemy.

Fairytales such as *Little Red Riding Hood* and *Three Little Pigs* depicted the wolf as evil. Robert Browning went further in his poem, Ivan Ivanovitch, in which he describes a horse-drawn sleigh full of people being chased by wolves. To survive the attack the adults throw their children to the wolves.

The literary slaughter of wolves took on physical dimensions in 10th century England, when King Edward accepted wolf heads in payment for taxes. Laws were passed allowing the extermination of wolves under the pretext of livestock protection. Around 1743 the last wolf in Britain was killed in Scotland and just over 30 years later Ireland's wolves succumbed to the same fate.

Above and right: Mans relationship with wolves has changed over the course of history. Once, this great predator was our friend and ally, before changes in our own circumstances led us to perceive wolves as sly, cunning killers that hid in the woods waiting to pounce on innocent and unwary children. Today, although perceptions are mixed, our understanding of the true nature of wolves has improved, and they are once more considered the icon of wilderness.

Prior to colonisation, in North America the wolf faired much better. Native Americans saw wolves as spiritual brothers. Wolves were revered as great hunters and looked up to by warriors, who adorned themselves in wolf skins so that they might absorb the wolf's legendary hunting skills.

However, the American wolf was living on borrowed time. As Europeans colonised the New World, they began to clear forests for fields and pastures useful for farming. In so doing, many of the wolf's natural prey were decimated and wolves began to attack domestic livestock to survive. With their European prejudices, the war against wolves had reached the American continent and, in 1860, the last wolf in New England was killed.

In the American west the persecution of wolves was no less ferocious. Thousands were slaughtered during the construction of roads and railways throughout the 1860s and 1870s. Professional wolf cullers (wolfers) were employed to rid the land of wolves, using any possible means. In 1884 Montana introduced a wolf bounty – $1 per wolf. By 1875 bounties on wolves had increased to $8 per head, and in 35 years hunters in Montana alone slaughtered 80,000 wolves.

In little over three centuries, man had slaughtered an estimated 250,000 wolves. Worldwide, in a single millennium, we had brought our once-close ally to the brink of extinction.

Above, right and overleaf: Wolves remain wary of humans and spend most of their lives avoiding us, populating habitats where human encroachment is limited. Armed with an exceptional sense of smell, keen hearing and good eyesight, wolves are typically aware of our presence long before we have even an inkling they're around, and disperse at the faintest whiff of man.

Taxonomy

There are three species of wolf and several sub-species. The most common, Canis lupus (grey wolf), is widely dispersed, with numerous sub-species. The red wolf *(Canis rufus)* is one of the rarest of the canid family and is found only in the US. The Ethiopian wolf *(Canis simensis)* inhabits a compact range in the mountains of Ethiopia.

Wolves are ideally adapted for surviving in most types of habitat and are at home equally on dry land, in snow, and in water.

Grey wolf *Canis lupus*

Classification of the grey wolf is difficult due, in part, to its wide and varied dispersal. The current, official classification is as shown below.

Current classification of North American grey wolves

Latin name	Common name	Range	Physical characteristics	Additional information
Canis lupus occidentalis	Mackenzie Valley wolf	Alaska and western Canada	The largest of all North American wolves ranging in colour from white to black	Sub-species include: *columbianus, griseoalbus, mackenzii, occidentalis, pambasileus and tundrarum.* Due to a wide and varied habitat and sub-species dispersal, these wolves are not considered endangered.
Canis lupus nubilus		Western US, north-eastern US, southeast Alaska and central and northeast Canada		Sub-species include: *beothucus, crassodon, fuscus, hudsonicus, irremotus, labradorius, ligoni, manningi, mogollenensis, monstrabilis and youngi.*
Canis lupus lycaon		South-eastern Canada		Some taxonomists argue that the wolves of eastern Canada, sometimes referred to as timber wolves, are worthy of a distinct classification.
Canis lupus arctos	Arctic wolf	The Canadian arctic islands and Greenland	Large and stocky build with white or cream colouring	Sub-species include: *bernardi and orion.*
Canis lupus baileyi	Mexican wolf (lobos)	South-west US and Mexico.	The smallest of the North American wolves and usually grey in colour.	Genetically distinct sub-specie that is thought to have become extinct in the late 20th century, although a small remnant population may remain in Mexico. Re-introduced to New Mexico and Arizona in 2000.

Opposite page: North American grey wolf
(Canis lupus), the most common and
widely dispersed of the tree wolf species.

There are several European, Middle Eastern, African and Asian sub-species, as shown below.

Current classification of European and Asian grey wolves

Latin name	Common name	Range	Physical characteristics	Additional information
Canis lupus albus	Tundra or Turukhan wolf	Northern Russia and northern Finland	Large wolves with light coloured fur Small in size (between 16 – 22kg) with thin, buff coloured pelage	
Canis lupus arabs	Arabian wolf	The Arabian peninsula		
Canis lupus cubanensis		Occurs between the Caspian sea and the Black sea		
Canis lupus communis		Occurring in the Ural mountains of north-central Siberia		
Canis lupus hattai or C.l. rex.		Region of Hokkaido, Japan		Thought to be extinct.
Canis lupus hodophilax		Honshu, Japan	Smaller than *C.l. hattai*, with short, smooth fur	Also extinct.
Canis lupus italicus	Italian wolf	Occurs in areas of Italy		
Canis lupus lupaster		Occurs in northern Egypt and Libya		This sub-specie was originally classified as a jackal.
Canis lupus	Common wolf	Found across Europe,central Asia,southern Russia, China, Mongolia and the Himalayan mountain region.	A medium-sized wolf with short, dense grey fur	The most common of theEuropean/Asian Grey wolves and the most likely to be seen in the wild.
Canis lupus pallipes		Occurs in India and further west into Iraq		

Above: The European grey wolf *(Canis lupus)*, like its North American cousin, is widely dispersed, although fewer in number.

Overleaf: Despite the name, grey wolves' pelage varies from all-white to all-black, depending on habitat. For example, in the frozen north of Canada, and in Alaska, all wolves within a pack may be white, helping them to blend with snowy terrain.

Red wolf *Canis rufus*

Around 1930 Canis rufus floridianus became extinct, followed by Canis rufus rufus, in the early 1970s. The remaining sub-species, Canis rufus gregregoryi, is believed to have become extinct in the wild circa 1980.

Ethiopian wolf *Canis simensis*

The Ethiopian wolf, found in isolated pockets in Ethiopia, is also known by several other names, including the Abyssinian wolf, Abyssinian jackal, Simien jackal, Simien fox and red jackal. Despite its close resemblance to the fox, studies have revealed a closer link to wolves, coyotes and jackals than was previously thought, resulting in classification by the IUCN as a species of wolf, thought to be descended from a grey wolf ancestor that migrated from western Europe or Russia at the close of the last ice age.

Grey wolf *Canis lupus*

The behaviour and natural history across all grey wolf sub-species are remarkably similar.

The body

Wolves are designed for endurance and speed. Comparatively long, thin legs propel the body through deep snow at speeds quicker than can be managed by the stouter legs of many prey species. The feet are large and, in crusted snow, act like snowshoes.

Most wolves reach adult proportions by the age of one year, with males around 20% larger than females. An average-sized male weighs 100 lbs (45 kg) and measures between 150 – 200 cm (60 – 78 in) from nose to tail (the tail accounting for about a quarter of the overall length). Females weigh about 80 lbs (36 kg) and are approximately 15 cm (6 in) less in length. In the far north of North America wolves may exceed 120 lbs (55 kg), and in Alaska a wolf weighing a heavyweight 175 lbs (79 kg) has been recorded.

The head

The head is designed to withstand the immense stresses placed on the jaw during a kill. Powerful muscles are attached to the lower section, which helps the animal maintain a firm grip on struggling prey. They have 42 teeth.

Senses

A wolf's sense of smell is thousands of times more sensitive than ours. The rostrum contains an estimated 280 million olfactory sensors that enable them to identify not only the presence of prey up to 2 miles (3 km) away, but also the prey's state of health. They can detect certain sounds from great distances, and their eyesight enables them to see in daylight and at night with a slightly advanced ability to focus using binocular vision.

Pelage

Fur colour changes with age and ranges from white to black, more commonly varying between cream, brown and a mix of tones. This colouring stems from a need for camouflage.

The surface coat is formed by long, coarse guard hairs, which provide not only colouring but also protection from rain and snow, and the wear and tear typical of life in a forest. Below the outer coat is a layer of under-fur that provides insulation and enables wolves to exist in extreme cold temperatures.

Red wolf *Canis rufus*

The red wolf is the smallest of the North American wolves. Their coats, which are much thinner than that of grey wolves, are predominantly grey, with a buff or rufous tinge to the upper body, sometimes overlaid with black. Although smaller than grey wolves, weighing around 65 lbs (30 kg) and standing up to 79 cm (31 in) at the shoulder, red wolves have larger ears, and longer legs in proportion to their body.

Top left: Wolves' heads are adapted to grasp, hold and pull down prey during a kill. Canines and incisors are used to first stab and then secure prey, while the pre-molars and carnassials are used to shear meat and to crunch bone to get at the marrow.

Top right: Wolves' legs are positioned close to the large, narrow chest, with toes turned outward, enabling them to step into their own tracks. This requires less energy output when moving across inhospitable terrain.

Bottom: Wolves' tracks are distinctive and reveal the structure of paws. Relatively, the feet are large and, in crusted snow, act like snowshoes by spreading the animals weight, preventing it from sinking too deeply.

Ethiopian wolf *Canis simensis*

Like the red wolf, the tail of this animal has a black tip. They are smaller than the grey wolf, being around 60cm (24 inches) at the shoulder and weighing around 18kg (40 pounds). Females are often up to 20% smaller than males.

Top: Smaller and with a different pelage than grey wolves, the Ethiopian wolf is adapted to the specific conditions and habitat of the Ethiopian mountains.

Below: Red wolves are the smallest of the North American wolf species and get their name from the buff or red tinge visible on the pelage. Despite their small size, legs and ears are proportionally larger than the grey wolf.

Opposite page: European wolves are distinctly similar to North American wolves, although pack size tends to be smaller due to the variation in diet. Their coat is typically a mix of greys and browns that helps them to blend in woodland and forest, the principle habitat of European wolves.

Habitat and distribution

GREY WOLF

Of all the Earth's habitats only two – rainforests and true deserts – are impervious to habitation by wolves. Wolves are extinct in some regions, including countries such as Japan, Mexico and the UK. In total there are an estimated 150,000 wolves worldwide.

Wolves need to move around to find prey, locate mates, raise pups and avoid danger. For this reason, urban development has played almost as significant a part in the depletion of populations as hunting and persecution. Wolves are more likely to inhabit public lands than private. Therefore, habitat selection is not based solely on avoiding humans but also a preference for natural landscapes and responses to variables such as vegetation.

Above: The distinctive track of a grey wolf, often the only sign of their presence we ever get to see.

Opposite page: Wolves are widely dispersed. They can survive extreme climates, ranging from some of the world's hottest to coldest environments. Only rainforest and true desert have remained impervious to habitation by wolves.

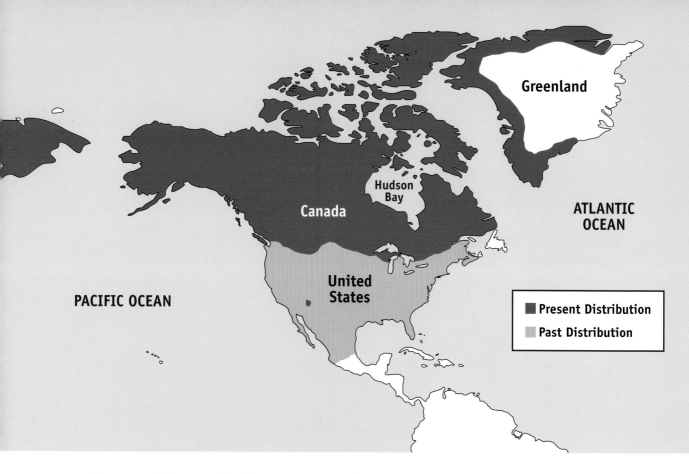

Grey wolf populations – Canada

Region	Estimated population	Status	Percentage of historical range still occupied
Alberta	4,000	Stable-decreasing	80%
British Columbia	8,000	Increasing	80%
Labrador	2,000	Stable	95%
Manitoba	4,000 – 6,000	Stable	70%
Northwest Territory	10,000	Stable	95%
Ontario	9,000	Stable	80%
Quebec	6,000	Stable	80%
Saskatchewan	5,000	Increasing	70%
Yukon	4,500	Stable	80%

Grey wolf populations – United States

Region	Estimated population	Status	Percentage of historical range still occupied
Alaska	5,000 – 8,000	Stable – increasing	95%
Idaho	15	Increasing	50%
Michigan	70	Increasing	15%
Minnesota	1,750 – 2,000	Increasing	30%
Montana	60 – 90	Increasing	15%
Washington	5	Increasing	5%
Wisconsin	55	Increasing	15%

Grey wolf populations – Europe, Middle East, Africa and Asia

Country	Estimated population	Percentage of historical range still occupied	Country	Estimated population	Percentage of historical range still occupied
Afghanistan	1,000	90%	Israel	100	60%
Albania	Unknown	Unknown	Italy	250	10%
Arabian peninsular	260	90%	Jordan	200	90%
Bangladesh	Unknown	Unknown	Lebanon	10	5%
Bhutan	Unknown	Unknown	Mongolia	10,000	95%
Bulgaria	500	30%	Nepal	Unknown	Unknown
China	Unknown	20%	Norway	5	2%
Czech Republic	50	10%	Pakistan	Unknown	Unknown
Egypt-Sinai	25	90%	Poland	850	90%
Finland	90	10%	Portugal	150	20%
France	5	5%	Romania	2,000	15%
Germany	5	5%	Slovac Republic	300	15%
Greece	500	60%	Spain	1,500	15%
Greenland	60	60%	Sweden	20	5%
Hungary	40	10%	Syria	300	10%
India	1,000	20%	Turkey	Unknown	Unknown
Iran	1,000	80%	Former USSR	90,000	65%
Iraq	Unknown	Unknown	Former Yugoslavia	500	45%

RED WOLF

Around 100 red wolves are roaming wild, descendants of 14 captive animals released in a controversial recovery effort, and can be found only in the Alligator River National Wildlife Refuge and the Pocosin Lakes area of North Carolina.

ETHIOPIAN WOLF

The critically endangered Ethiopian wolf is one of a remarkable collection of animals living above 3,000m (9,750 feet) on Ethiopian mountains. Because of habitat requirements the species is restricted to the afro-alpine (approx. 3,700-4,400m) and sub-alpine (approx. 3,000-3,700m) regions. There are five specific areas where the species is confirmed to occur in varying numbers: Simien Mountains, Mount Guna, north-eastern Shoa, the Arsi Mountains and the Bale Mountains.

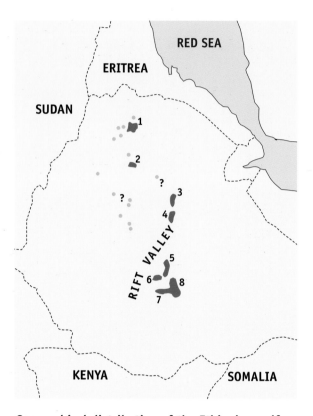

Geographical distribution of the Ethiopian wolf.
1: Simien Mountains National Park **2:** Mount Guna
3: Menz **4:** Ankober **5:** Arsi Mountains
6: Mount Kenya **7:** Somkaro/Korduro Mountains
8: Bale Mountains National Park.
●: Indicate records prior to 1925.
?: Indicate uncertain or unconfirmed recoreds.

Ethiopian wolf populations

Region	Estimated population
Simien Mountains	20-40
Mount Guna	less than 20
North-eastern Shoa	50-75
Arsi Mountains	80-160
Bale Mountains (including Bale Mountains National Park)	460-510

Opposite page, top: Wolves tend to thrive in whatever habitat they find themselves. In ancient times, wolves were numerous from Mexico to the Arctic, from northern Norway to the tip of Spain, in the Middle East and northern Africa, and from southern India to Japan.

Opposite page, bottom: Wolves need space: to move around in order to find prey, locate mates, raise pups and avoid danger. For this reason, urban development has played almost as significant a part in the depletion of populations as hunting and persecution.

Above and overleaf: Natural features such as rivers often form the boundaries of a pack's territory.

Right: Habitat selection is not based solely on avoiding humans but also a preference for natural landscapes and responses to variables such as vegetation.

Opposite page: Contrary to logical assumption, prey density is less a deciding factor in wolf distribution. Certain studies have found little to no difference in prey densities in habitats where wolves exist compared to those where they don't. It seems that more than anything wolves simply love wilderness.

Life in the pack

Wolf packs operate within highly developed social structures where the strength and survival of the group takes precedence over any individual. Pack sizes vary between around two and 20 wolves, depending on age and available territory.

Types of prey also influence pack size. Where wolves feed primarily on small mammals, such as in desert regions, pack sizes tend to be small. However, in Alaska and Canada, where wolves prey on large ungulates, pack sizes can exceed 20.

Above: The call of the wild – wolves use a sophisticated form of language to communicate within and outside of the pack.

Opposite page: Daily activity includes territory management – the remarking of boundaries and borders, and the assessment of prey activity.

PACK STRUCTURE

A pack is formed when a male and female join to mate, the offspring of the union remaining within the unit. Although outsiders can be accepted into a pack, typically a pack is made up entirely of related individuals.

The dominant wolves are the mating pair, referred to as alpha wolves. Next in line is the beta male, whose role is to reinforce the will of the alpha male and act as stand-in parent in the absence of the alpha pair. The roles of the remaining subordinate wolves are equally critical to pack survival and change over time. In general they perform community duties, such as territory management, finding food and babysitting.

At the bottom of the hierarchical pyramid is the omega wolf, the lowest ranking member of the pack. Often this individual is picked on by all other wolves and frequently relies for food on leftover scraps.

Top: The offspring of the union of the alpha male and female typically remain within the pack. It is not unusual for a pack to consist entirely of related individuals.

Middle: Wolves are very caring parents and all pack members undertake babysitting duties. The bonds created during wolves' early lives remain throughout and are cemented during periods of social interaction.

Bottom: Within the unit a strict hierarchical structure is observed. The dominant wolves are the alpha pair. Their roles and the continuity of their leadership are central to the success of the pack. Next in line is the beta male.

Opposite page: Within two weeks of birth pups open their eyes. A week later they grow milk teeth explore inside the den, before making short, external sojourns about two weeks later. By the age of two months pups are weaned and regularly travel to rendezvous sites. A month later they begin to travel with the pack.

Overleaf: Within the pack discipline is strictly maintained using physical and non-physical signs, such as growls and snarls, body posture and bites.

Discipline within the pack is strictly maintained, as I was to witness while photographing wolves in Minnesota. Two wolves sniffed at my face and began to lick my mouth, but as the two leaders welcomed me into the pack, close by and unknown to me, a young male wolf crept closer until he was directly behind me and I felt a nip on my back. Recognising the situation the alpha male pulled away from me and snapped at the mischievous youth, herding him towards the trees and backing him into a corner. I watched as the dominant wolf, growling audibly, chastised the wayward intruder with soft bites to the nose, a typical form of discipline.

As the pack matures the positions of individuals change. Subordinate wolves constantly battle to assert their place in the pecking order. At some point the alpha male and female will perish and a previously subordinate wolf will win the alpha role. Although the alpha male can be challenged from within the pack or by an outsider, it's a surprisingly rare occurrence.

Opposite page: During feeding emotions run high and conflict between subordinate wolves in particular is likely. In the image at top, notice the omega wolf cowering at the rear of this feeding pack, waiting for the leftover scraps.

Above: Soft bites to the nose are a typical form of discipline within the pack. Also notice the subordinate body posture of the lesser wolf.

LEADERSHIP

All wolves have individual character traits. Alpha males may rule with brute force and aggression, or take a more subtle approach. Although the alpha male is the leader of the pack, leadership responsibilities are frequently shared.

The role of the alpha female is twofold: to produce offspring and to regulate reproduction in other females in the pack. More often than not to die, alpha females leave a pack rather than having the opportunity to die in position.

BEHAVIOUR AND INTERACTION

Teamwork is essential to pack survival and practically all wolf behaviour is designed to promote social harmony and security. As well as auditory communication, visual displays are used in face-to-face encounters. If clarification of intention is needed, wolves use a repertoire of sounds.

A large proportion of wolf behaviour is associated with establishing a pecking order, and the interplay of these forces creates a balance within the group that keeps the pack stable.

Previous page: Subordinate wolves battle constantly to assert their place in the hierarchy. Although this behaviour can appear overly aggressive at times, rarely does it lead to physical harm. When greeting after spells away from the pack, touch and physical proximately is assuring to both the returning wolves, relieved to be back within the safety of the unit, and the welcoming party, happy at the encounter with friend not foe.

Above: Although the alpha male is the dominant wolf, leadership responsibilities are shared. For example, it is a frequent occurrence for a subordinate wolf to lead a hunt.

Left; The role of the alpha female is to produce offspring and to regulate reproduction within the pack.

Opposite page:In face-to-face encounters wolves use a mix of visual, auditory and tactile communication. The combination of different types of communication enforces and clarifies the message.

FRIENDLY BEHAVIOUR

When two wolves meet they engage in social investigation, which involves smelling the nose, face and genitals to determine between friend and foe. During sniffing, the subordinate wolf holds its tail between its legs in an act of submission, while the dominant animal raises its tail. A more intimate behaviour is snuffling, where one individual places its nose through the neck fur of another, gently touching the skin beneath.

When soliciting affection, grooming or food, a wolf will instinctively lift its paw, perhaps accompanied with a high-pitched whining or whimpering. When insisting on affection, particularly in pups, wolves use a tactic known as snout bunting – pushing upward with their snout against another wolf's chin.

SOCIAL INTERACTION

Play is incredibly important and a key component of pack stability. Typically, a play session is preceded by play-invitation signals and takes the form of chasing, ambushing and mock fighting

Right: Snuffling – placing the nose through the neck fur of another wolf – is a particularly intimate behavioural trait.

Opposite page: Like domestic dogs, when clamouring affection, grooming or food, wolves will typically lift their front paw.

Above: Standing across is a tactile form of low-intensity domination behaviour displayed by wolves.

Left: Riding up, where the dominant wolf places its legs on the back of the lesser wolf, is another form of low intensity threat.

Opposite page: The bite threat is a form of high-intensity threat often displayed between conflicting subordinate adults.

Overleaf: The tale held firmly between the legs (front wolf) is a sign of submission against an aggressor or aggressors. This scene is indicative of an ambush, a form of high-intensity threat displayed by wolves.

LOW-INTENSITY THREAT

When involving an overtly dominant wolf conflict, behaviour may be nothing more than a low-intensity threat, whereby the dominant animal simply draws itself to its full height, raises its tail and stares intently at the subordinate.

More tactile forms of low-intensity threat behaviour are standing across, where the dominant wolf straddles the back of the submissive animal, which may in turn lick the underbelly of the aggressor; and riding up, which involves the dominant wolf placing its front legs on the back of the lesser animal, possibly soft biting the scruff of the neck simultaneously.

HIGH-INTENSITY THREAT

Within the pack, high-intensity threats are most likely between subordinate wolves. A common form of this more aggressive behaviour is the bite threat. The initiating wolf will hold its head high and arch its neck. The wolf will open its mouth and retract its lips to display its menacing canine teeth. Another, less overt form of high-intensity threat is the ambush, where one wolf will crouch low, much like a leopard, and surprise its victim.

PASSIVE AND ACTIVE SUBMISSION

In submission, a wolf may revert to active submission (as displayed during a friendly encounter) or, when seriously outranked or threatened by many wolves, it may adopt a more passive approach, rolling onto its back with its tail between its legs and splaying its legs to present its genital region.

DEFENSIVE THREATS

If attempts at submission fail to appease an aggressor or aggressors, a wolf may resort to defensive threats. The defending wolf will arch its back, hold its head and ears back and curve its tail down. Teeth will be bared, sometimes snapping, and the wolf will growl or bark. However, it averts its eyes in a submissive gesture.

Top and bottom: Defensive threats – arched back with head and ears held back, and teeth bared – are used when other submissive tactics have failed to appease an aggressor.

Opposite page: When seriously outranked a lesser wolf may revert to passive submission, rolling onto its back and splaying its legs to present the genital region.

HOW WOLVES COMMUNICATE

Wolves communicate on several levels, spanning all the senses. From behavioural studies we can also assess that messages are liable to misinterpretation, which can lead to conflict.

SOUND

In close proximity, adult wolves use a mix of harmonic and noisy vocalisations. Harmonic sounds include yelps, whines and whimpers and are associated with friendly or submissive behaviour. Conversely, noisy sounds, such as growls, woofs, barks and snarls, are linked to aggressive and domineering behaviour.

Howling, the sound most greatly associated with wolves, is a long distance call with three main purposes. Within the pack it is used to call together separated group members or simply as a means of identification and assessing location. Howls also inform neighbouring packs of the presence of a rival pack. The final reason wolves howl is that they seem to enjoy it.

The ability of wolves to communicate over long distances is affected by external factors, such as weather, competing noise and habitat.

Opposite page: Wolves use several means of communication, including that most closely associated with the species – howling.

Above: Howling has three main purposes: to call together dispersed pack members, to identify pack members and location, and to inform neighbouring packs of a rival pack's presence.

Right: Typically a single wolf initiates a chorus howl. A second wolf joins in before others follow. No two wolves howl in the same pitch and if you were to replicate the pitch of one wolf it would quickly switch. One reason for this is to allow listening wolves to count the number of wolves involved, an indication of pack size.

SMELL

The exact sources of wolf odours are difficult to identify but it's thought they emanate from various skin and bodily glands, including those associated with hair follicles (sebaceous glands), the face, lips and back (apocrine glands), and the foot, in particular the pads and between the toes (eccrine, or true sweat glands).

The most obvious form of scent communication is urination, which, despite variances in composition, is individually identifiable. Scent and scent marking convey numerous messages, including information on species, individual id, age, gender, social rank and reproductive status.

Recognition is a key element of olfactory communication whether it's passive, informing other wolves it's a friend, or domineering, identifying social status or the boundaries of a territory.

The importance of territorial marking is obvious from the amount of time and effort wolves put into it. Boundary marking is done during patrols with scent marks made at regular intervals throughout the territory. Given that wolves' territory can extend beyond 5,000 square miles, this is no mean feat.

Above: Scent marking is used to mark the boundary of a territory, and the scent from urine conveys significant information to other wolves.

Opposite page; Recognition is a key factor of communication via smell. Pups use smell to recognise their mother. Adults use it to distinguish between friend and foe.

SCENT ROLLING

Wolves find much enjoyment in rolling around in putrid smelling substances, such as rotted carcasses and faeces. Familiarisation with unknown smells or concealment of individual odours is one possible reason. Another suggestion is that it's used as a form of perfume.

VISUAL COMMUNICATION

Combined with other forms of communication, such as sound and smell, visual messages help clarify intent and meaning, particularly when in close proximity. In general, visual signals identify between one continuum and another simultaneously.

TOUCH

In newborn pups, touch is vital for reassurance and to bond with siblings and parents. Between adults, tactile communication revolves around friendly behaviour and is common between greeting pack members and mates as a means of reducing levels of stress, as well as during pack ceremonies and displays of courtship. In aggressive situations tactile communication is used typically as a last resort.

Below: Scent rolling is a particularly enjoyable habit of wolves. The exact reason for scent rolling is unknown but it's thought to be a form of familiarization or concealment of odour.

Opposite page: Touch plays a vital part in a young pups life. Through tactile communication they gain reassurance and bonding with parents and siblings.

TERRITORY MANAGEMENT

In general wolves are highly territorial, although it's not uncommon for them to display nomadic-like tendencies. Because existing territories remain occupied indefinitely, forming packs must seek new territories wherever they can find a suitable habitat, either in an abandoned territory or an unoccupied site.

The principal influences on territory location are the type and habits of prey species, as well as their movements. Sedentary prey species having relatively small home ranges, may provide sufficient food for wolves to manage similarly small, fixed territories. Where the main prey species migrate long distances, such as Arctic caribou, wolves tend to follow the herd and be less territorial. Territory size is also influenced by altitude and productivity, being smaller at low altitude where prey is in greater abundance and hunting is easier.

Observations of wolves indicate that they plan ahead and set territory size based on expected pack size over time, allowing for offspring.

Wolves travel throughout their territory in single file, spreading out only in bare terrain, and use ready-formed trails, as well as gravel bars, ridges, roads and frozen waterways. Occasionally, where needs arise, wolves travel outside the territory, principally during dispersal when seeking a mate and locating a new territory. Another, more hazardous reason for extraterritorial travel is to find food. This can mean trespassing on another pack's territory, placing them in potential conflict.

Top: Scent emanates from wolves' feet, particularly the eccrine glands found between the toes and on the pads. Scent is used to mark the boundary of a territory and to communicate.

Opposite page, top: Wolves move around their territory in single file, typically using well-worn tracks.

Right: When moving into the open, wolves will spread out rather than move in single file.

DIET

Within their territory wolves have preferred prey. In any given habitat wolves eat anything from fruit and vegetation, insects, rodents and small mammals, to large ungulates, such as caribou and moose. They prefer to prey on large animals that, although dangerous to kill, are more efficient physiologically.

Geography plays a defining role in what constitutes wolves' primary food source. For example, in the boreal and coniferous forests of Canada, northern Scandinavia and Russia, moose represent the predominant prey. Where moose are present, wolves also feed on roe deer, red deer, elk and white-tailed deer, while musk oxen and Dall's sheep compliment a diet of caribou. Eurasian wolves from west Scandinavia and northern Europe to India, China and Mongolia commonly prey on myriad species including wild boar, European bison, saiga antelope, ibex, chamois, mountain goats, fallow, musk and sika deer, gazelles and bactrian camels. In more specialised habitats wolves are not afraid to try local delicacies.

Opposite page: Although essentially carnivorous, wolves eat a varied diet that can contain anything from fruit and vegetation, insects and small mammals, as well as large ungulates.

Top: In coastal regions wolves have been known to feast on a diet of salmon, which is readily available during the annual salmon migration.

Bottom: In northern Europe, red deer form a staple of wolves' diet.

HUNTING AND PREDATION

Wolves are good hunters, and regularly attack and kill prey up to ten times their own size. In hunting, prey must first be located, necessitating travelling throughout the territory, visiting prey-rich areas and previous kill sites. Wolves appear to use memory and experience extensively when embarking on a hunt. Typically, prey is detected first by smell, followed by visual confirmation.

Wolves pass many individual animals seemingly oblivious to their presence and rarely, if ever, kill at random. They test potential prey by giving chase and, as the prey flee or scatter, the wolves seek to identify weaknesses in an individual. As well as weak and injured animals, wolves also single out older individuals that are in poor condition and less able to defend themselves. During the birthing season they also target newborn calves and fawns.

Once prey is selected, the main pursuit begins. In general, wolves attack in pairs or groups. When going in for the kill one wolf will bite on the prey's nose, dragging its head down and immobilising it. The remaining wolves attack the hindquarters, cutting and tearing at the muscles and tendons.

Massive blood loss causes the prey animal to go into shock, and once the kill is made the alpha pair assume first pickings.

Above and right: A wolf in northern Canada stalks and attacks a caribou. Caribou form the staple diet of wolves in this region of North America.

MATING, REPRODUCTION AND GROWING UP

Wolves reach sexual maturity around the age of two years and the mating season lasts between January and April. Where the alpha pair dominates, lower-ranking wolves that risk mating are likely to receive an aggressive repost and the possibility of being ostracised or expelled.

Courtship begins with a period of bonding and the mating wolves may separate temporarily from the pack. The pair sleeps close together and, when approaching, make quiet whining sounds, touch noses, rub bodies and muzzle each other's rostrums. Mutual grooming is commonplace and touching almost constant.

As courtship progresses, the male will test the female's receptiveness by sniffing the genital region and scenting the air for signs of oestrus, which lasts for around one week. The male mounts the female from behind and, once inserted, the male's penis swells, while simultaneously the female's vaginal wall constricts, literally tying the pair together. Gestation takes around 63 days and prior to giving birth the female will find a den, typically in a hollow in a bank. A den is usually formed with a long entrance tunnel leading to a compact, elevated birthing chamber, which enables the mother to detect approaching predators.

Top: Courting wolves often separate from the pack temporarily to bond. Bonding takes the form of tactile communication, including touching noses, nuzzling and body rubbing.

Bottom: Mating occurs with the male mounting the female from behind. When inserted the penis swells, while the females vaginal wall contracts, literally holding the pair together.

Opposite page, top: Pups are born blind and deaf and spend the early part of their lives tucked away safely in the den.

Opposite page, bottom: The alpha male is very protective of the den site.

Pups are born blind and deaf but have an acute sense of smell. Immediately after birth the female will lick away and eat the foetal sac, allowing the pup to takes its first breath. She will then sever the umbilical cord and consume the placenta. Once pups are born, the alpha male is very protective of the den site and acts to divert potential predators, such as bears and eagles, with decoy tactics.

Non-mating females produce milk and help with feeding, while males vie for babysitting rights. Pack members also bring food for the mother, as well as the pups, once they are able to eat meat. Pup mortality is around 30% – 60%.

PACK EVOLUTION

Around 75% of surviving wolves disperse by the age of three years. On leaving a pack, wolves may travel great distances for long periods before settling down. Others immigrate to an existing pack.

Within an existing pack, social hierarchy is constantly changing among the lower-ranking wolves. The alpha male will remain dominant so long as he commands obedience from subordinates and can defend his status against an intruder. The status of the alpha female is typically less secure. Other females within the pack vie to mate with the alpha male and it is only a strong, dominant alpha female that will resist. It's usual for an alpha female to relinquish her position within two years.

Opposite page, top: Between the ages of 4-6 weeks the pups begin to emerge from the den. However, it will be another 4 weeks before they begin to venture very far from the security the den provides.

Opposite page, bottom: Play forms an important part of pups' development. Siblings use this period to learn about social structure, discipline and the hunting tactics that will help them to survive in later life.

Top: Pups feed on their mother's milk for the first two months of their life.

Bottom: Pup mortality is high, varying between 30-60% depending on the strength of the pack, the availability of food and the climate.

Wolves in their environment

The presence of wolves not only helps to manage populations of ungulates and other prey species, but also positively affects the well being of native flora and fauna.

Common factors in the physiology of animals are that predators are adapted to hunt and kill, while prey species have evolved to defend and flee. In the wolf habitat, prey animals possess a combination of physical attributes and behavioural traits to aid survival.

Landscape features also provide defences for prey. Water can slow wolves sufficiently for naturally aquatic animals to escape. In mountainous and rocky regions, elevation enables sheep and goats to evade hunting wolves.

Opposite page and above: The presence of wolves has a positive effect on native flora and fauna. In its element the wolf is at the top of the food chain and, as with most regions where mega-fauna exist, the state of biodiversity is often reflected in the condition of its primary predator.

Right: Wolves are considered mega-fauna and sit at the top of the natural food chain.

Below: In much of their range, grey wolves compete with brown bears for prey, and may fall prey to the bears. Brown bears are a particular threat to wolf cubs.

Top: In mountainous and rocky regions elevation helps prey species such as mountain goats to evade the wolf.

Below: Landscape features, such as rivers, form natural defences for some prey species. Although wolves are at home in water, water slows their speed, allowing prey to escape.

EFFECTS OF WOLF PREDATION

It would be logical to think that where wolf populations were both numerous and dense, prey species would be diminished. However, the reality is more complex and, perhaps, surprising.

Prey populations are affected as much by the ability to re-populate as they are by predation. As such, prey populations are dependent on plentiful food, as well as external influences, such as the weather. An abundance of food leads to stronger, fitter animals, while mild winters also improve survival rates. The presence of other large predators also alters the effect of predation by wolves.

Above: Coyotes regularly scavenge on wolf kills and encounters between the two species are common in certain parts of North America.

Left: There is an old Inuit saying: "It is the wolf that makes the caribou strong". On the whole, prey species benefit from the presence of wolves, which take out weaker animals allowing the strong to thrive.

Opposite page, top: In the winter months, wolves in North America are likely to encounter mountain lions. Wolf/big cat encounters also occur elsewhere, such as Europe and Asia, where wolves share territory with tigers and lynx, in particular.

Opposite page, bottom: Wolves often scavenge on Black bear kills and pose a threat to the bear's cubs. The relationship between wolves and black bears is typically a reversal of their relationship with brown bears.

COMPETITION BETWEEN PREDATORS

Wolves share their environment with numerous other predators. In most instances, encounters occur at a kill site, where the wolves are scavenging on another predator's kill or vice versa. The greatest competition is with brown bears, which share an almost identical range to wolves and are undaunted in approaching wolves feeding on a carcass. In most cases it's likely that the bear will win the day and steal the carcass.

Brown bears also pose a threat to wolf pups if stumbling across an unattended den.

During encounters between American black bears and wolves, roles are typically reversed. In encounters over food, wolves are likely to overrun the bear and make off with the scavenged prey. Wolves have also been known to seek the dens of black bears to prey on cubs.

The other major predator that wolves may encounter is the mountain lion (cougar/puma), particularly in winter when prey moves into habitat more suited to the big cat. Wolf/tiger encounters also occur in Russia and, to a much lesser extent, in India. Wolves and Eurasian lynx also inhabit the same habitat. Of canid species, wolves regularly encounter coyotes, which frequently scavenge at kill sites. Outside North America wolves may encounter dholes (Asiatic wild dog), striped hyenas and golden jackals, while in Poland there are records of wolves killing and eating raccoon dogs.

SYMBIOSIS WITH RAVENS

Of all the non-prey species that wolves encounter they appear to share a special relationship with ravens. These birds interact with wolves very differently than they do with other species to the extent that it is safe to assume that ravens can accurately differentiate between wolves, coyotes and foxes.

Ravens often follow hunting wolves in the hope of a scavenged meal. Evidence also suggests that ravens will alert wolves to the presence of an undiscovered carcass, with the benefit that wolves can tear through the thick outer hide impervious to ravens' bills, opening up the rich pickings within.

Right: Wolves and ravens appear to share a special relationship, with ravens often following a wolf pack hoping for a scavenged meal. The relationship also appears mutually beneficial; the presence of ravens alerting the wolves to a carcass.

Wolves and humans

Man's relationship with the wolf goes back thousands of years. It is a relationship that has fluctuated between adoration and almost obsessive idolisation, and hatred and loathing. The wolf, once trustful and respectful, has learned to fear humans and, in most areas, they avoid contact wherever possible.

The beginning of man's initial change in attitude was likely our development as a species from hunter, when we shared many values with wolves, to farmer, when the wolf became a pest and a threat to livestock and livelihoods.

As humans increasingly populated and farmed areas of wilderness – and thus wolf territories – the natural prey of wolves diminished and man and wolf were brought closer together. The result was hungry wolves in close proximity to human settlements with little or no natural prey. The consequence was attacks on livestock, the only food around, and our antipathy towards wolves was cemented.

Opposite page: Wolves and humans may share the same tracks but the relationship is an uneasy one.

Above: Today, for every wolf advocate there is an antagonist who would happily see the wolf dead as alive. Our preconception of wolves, however, is often drawn from ignorance, and strides made in our knowledge and understanding of wolves has helped protect them and the wilderness.

ATTACKS ON HUMANS

Wolves have killed humans but the extent to which killing occurs has been massively exaggerated. Historical records also indicate that a number of attacks accredited to wild wolves were actually made by tamed wolves, wolf-dog hybrids, wild dogs or rabid wolves. Other records from the 15th – 20th centuries suggest that wolf attacks on humans increased after conflicts and wars, perhaps because wolves became accustomed to feeding on corpses they encountered on battlefields. In all, European and north Asian records indicate that wolf attacks are very rare and generally occur under unusual circumstances.

Opposite page: Much of the knowledge we have gained about wolves has derived from the reintroduction of wolves to Yellowstone National Park in the US. Studies of packs such as Druid Pack, shown here, have opened our eyes to the sophisticated nature of wolves.

CONSERVATION AND CONTROL

As our knowledge of wolves has increased and replaced our long-held beliefs and prejudices, wolf conservation has grown to be a concern for both biologists and the general public. By the mid-1960s many of the bounties paid in the US on wolves were stopped, while attitudes in Europe also changed and wolf conservation programs were set up in a number of countries.

An understanding has also grown among scientists and conservationists that, in order to protect the wolf and nurture positive attitudes towards co-existence, a broad approach to conservation is needed that includes occasional control of wolf populations.

Much work is now being done in assessing and monitoring wolf numbers and ranges. Where necessary, habitat improvements can be made to assist wolf conservation, such as the reintroduction of prey species where numbers have fallen.

Numerous countries have also signed international agreements related to wolf conservation and established local, national and international treaties to co-ordinate management strategies. Restrictions on hunting of large game have been enforced, helping to sustain the availability of prey in wolf-inhabited areas.

YELLOWSTONE'S WOLVES

The world's most conspicuous wolf conservation programme began in the mid-1990s when scientists instigated the reintroduction of wolves to America's oldest national park. Prior to their reintroduction, Yellowstone National Park lost its last wolves in 1926. Fourteen wolves, captured in Alberta, Canada, were released into Yellowstone on two separate occasions early in 1995, after a period in an acclimatisation pen. Around a year later, following the same process, a further 17 wolves were relocated from British Columbia. In total 41 wolves were re-introduced to Yellowstone from diverse genetic stock. Collaring of Yellowstone's wolves continues annually, with around half of pups born collared and, where possible, re-collaring of the alpha pair.

Records indicate that the overall population of wolves in Yellowstone has grown steadily since 1995. The numbers equate to a five-fold increase in population and a tripling of area inhabited by wolves.

Much of what we know about wolves today emanates from the Yellowstone wolf re-introduction programme, from which biologists have learned much about how wolf populations evolved, the interaction and social behaviour of packs, the reproductive cycle and the individuality of single wolves.

Right: Druid Pack in Yellowstone National Park in the USA. Yellowstone is one of the best destinations for reliable wild wolf sightings.

Overleaf: Winter is often the best time for spotting wild wolves in America's Yellowstone National Park.

Wolf watching

HOW AND WHERE TO SEE WILD WOLVES

Wolves are elusive in the wild, distrusting of humans and quick to disperse when our presence is detected, and where wolves are abundant the habitat is often hostile and remote, making visiting these areas difficult, time-consuming and costly.

The best and possibly the only reliable location for wild wolf watching is Yellowstone National Park, in the US. Arguably, the most productive area for wolf sightings is the Lamar Valley, about a mile east of Soda Butte Cone through to the final turnout before the Lamar Canyon (Fisherman's).

Roosevelt Lodge is a popular base in the park, although its season is short (mid-June – early-September). Silvergate and Cooke City have good lodging, and camping is available at nearby Pebble Creek and Slough Creek campgrounds. The Slough Creek area, from the campground road entrance through Little America to the Yellowstone Picnic area is another productive wolf viewing area.

Above: Wolves are elusive in the wild, which makes wolf watching a difficult and often-frustrating task. Yellowstone National Park offers good opportunities to see wild wolves, while elsewhere captive wolves can be seen at conservation centres such as the Highland Wildlife Park in Scotland, and the International Wolf Centre in Ely, Minnesota.

Opposite page: A North American timber wolf at the Highland Wildlife Park in Kincraig, Scotland.

Winter is the prime season for seeing wolves, although Yellowstone winters can be viciously cold. Sightings are most likely to occur at dawn and dusk, with the best sightings typically between 6:00am and 10:00am. July and August are months to avoid, being hot and a time when elk and wolves migrate to higher, less accessible elevations.

ETHICS AND SAFETY

Keep noise levels to a minimum and avoid disturbing the animals. Children should be supervised at all times. Stay clear of carcasses and, in the unlikely event that a wolf approaches, remain calm, step away slowly and don't encourage interaction. Never run.

PHOTOGRAPHY TIPS

In most situations you will be photographing wolves from a fair distance away and so a long telephoto lens of 500mm plus is preferable. Alternatively, a shorter focal length lens with a teleconverter will achieve similar results. With such lenses it is essential to use a tripod for support and to avoid image blur caused by camera shake.

In Winter beware of cold temperatures affecting camera and battery performance. When light levels are low, as they often are given the time of day, season and climate, you may be photographing at the edge of the camera's exposure capabilities, using wide apertures and long shutter speeds. To gain greater flexibility over exposure settings, use a fast film or digital ISO-E rating such as ISO 400 or 800. For the best pictures, maximise composition by identifying and focusing on particular behavioural traits, body language or facial expressions, and watch for those moments above and beyond recording mere record shots of individual animals.

Wolf facts

CLASSIFICATION

Class: Mammalia

Order: Carnivora

Family: Canidae

Genus: Canis

Scientific names: *Canis lupus, Canis rufus* and *Canis simensis*

PHYSIOLOGY (average):

Length (including tail):

Males 150-200 cm (60-78 inches)

Females 140-185 cm (55-72 inches)

Height (at shoulder): 65-80 cm (26-32 inches)

Weight:

Males 43-48 kg (95-105 lbs)

Females 36-42 kg (80-90 lbs)

Variations: wolves in the south of a range are typically smaller than those in the north.

ECOLOGY

Gestation period: 61-64 days

Litter size: 1-11 pups, typically 4-6 pups

Dispersal age: 5-60 months, typically 20-26 months

Life span: Maximum 12 years in the wild

Predation: approximately 18 adult white-tailed deer, or 16 adult female caribou, or four adult and five calf moose per year, per wolf.

Other Wildlife Monographs titles published by

Evans Mitchell Books

www.embooks.co.uk

Wildlife Monographs
Snow Monkeys
ISBN: 978-1-901268-37-9

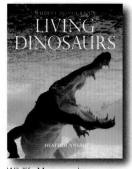

Wildlife Monographs
Living Dinosaurs
ISBN: 978-1-901268-36-2

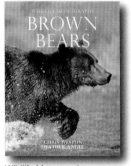

Wildlife Monographs
Brown Bears
ISBN: 978-1-901268-50-8

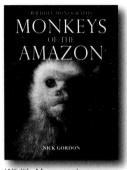

Wildlife Monographs
Monkeys of the Amazon
ISBN: 978-1-901268-10-2

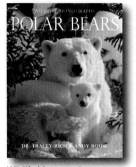

Wildlife Monographs
Polar Bears
ISBN: 978-1-901268-15-7

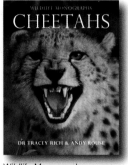

Wildlife Monographs
Cheetahs
ISBN: 978-1-901268-09-6

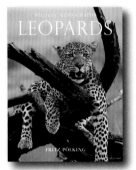

Wildlife Monographs
Leopards
ISBN: 978-1-901268-12-6

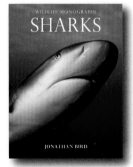

Wildlife Monographs
Sharks
ISBN: 978-1-901268-11-9

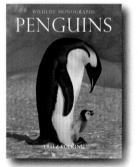

Wildlife Monographs
Penguins
ISBN: 978-1-901268-14-0

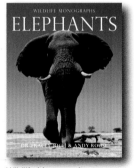

Wildlife Monographs
Elephants
ISBN: 978-1-901268-08-9

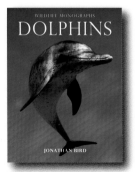

Wildlife Monographs
Dolphins
ISBN: 978-1-901268-17-1

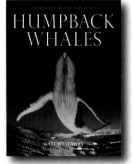

Wildlife Monographs
Humpback Whales
ISBN: 978-1-901268-56-0

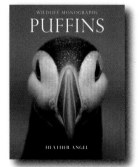

Wildlife Monographs
Puffins
ISBN: 978-1-901268-19-5

Wildlife Monographs
Giant Pandas
ISBN: 978-1-901268-13-3